My World of Science

HUMAN GROWTH

Angela Royston

D1297964

Heinemann Library
Chicago Illinois

© 2003 Heinemann Library
a division of Reed Elsevier Inc.
Chicago, Illinois

Customer Service 888-454-2279

Visit our website at www.heinemannlibrary.com

Designed by Jo Hinton-Malivoire and Tinstar Design Limited
Originated by Blenheim Colour, Ltd.
Printed and bound in China by South China Printing Company
Photo research by Maria Joannou and Sally Smith

07 06
10 9 8 7 6 5 4

Library of Congress Cataloging-in-Publication Data

Royston, Angela.
   Human growth / Angela Royston.
      p. cm. – (My world of science)
Summary: Explains in simple text how the human body grows.
Includes bibliographical references and index.
   ISBN 1-40340-989-7 (HC), 1-40343-196-5 (Pbk)
   1. Human growth–Juvenile literature. [1. Growth.] I. Title.
   QP84 .R78 2003
   612.6–dc21
                         2002009431

Acknowledgments
The author and publishers are grateful to the following for permission to reproduce copyright material: pp. 4, 5, 6, 8, 12, 13, 15, 17, 22, 24, 25, 26, 27, 29 Trevor Clifford; p. 7 PhotoDisc; p. 9 Science Photo Library/BSIP, Laurent; pp. 10, 20 Powerstock; p. 11 Greg Evans International; p. 14 Harcourt Education; p. 16 Science Photo Library; p. 18 Science Photo Library/BSIP Chassenet; p. 19 Robert Harding Picture Library; p. 21 Jenny Matthews/Network; p. 23 Pictor International; p. 28 Science Photo Library/BSIP, LECA.

Cover photograph reproduced with permission of Ace Photo Agency.

Some words are shown in bold, **like this.** You can find out what they mean by looking in the glossary.

Contents

Growing Bigger

When you were born, you were a tiny baby. You grew bigger and heavier until you reached the size you are now.

You will continue to grow for all the time you are a child. Sometimes you will grow faster. When you stop growing, you will be a "grown-up"!

Changing Size

Babies are different sizes when they are born. This baby is smaller than the teddy bear.

Babies and **toddlers** grow fast. Most three-year-old children are more than half the **height** of their **parents.**

Changing Weight

As well as growing taller, you get heavier. When you were born, you probably weighed less than this bottle of water.

You weigh a lot more now. This girl is being weighed by the school nurse. The nurse checks that she weighs about the right amount for her age.

Changing Shape

Your body changes shape as you grow. A baby's head is big compared to the rest of its body. Its arms and legs are short.

A **child's** arms and legs grow faster than the rest of its body. When you are about six years old, your legs are nearly half your **height.**

How Tall Will You Grow?

Children grow at different rates. So some children are taller or smaller than other children. The girl in red is taller than the boy and the other girl.

When you grow up, you will probably be about the same height as your **parents.** If your parents are medium **height,** you probably will be too.

Bones

Bones are hard and strong. They give your body its shape. Without bones, you would flop like jelly. Your bones grow longer and thicker as you grow.

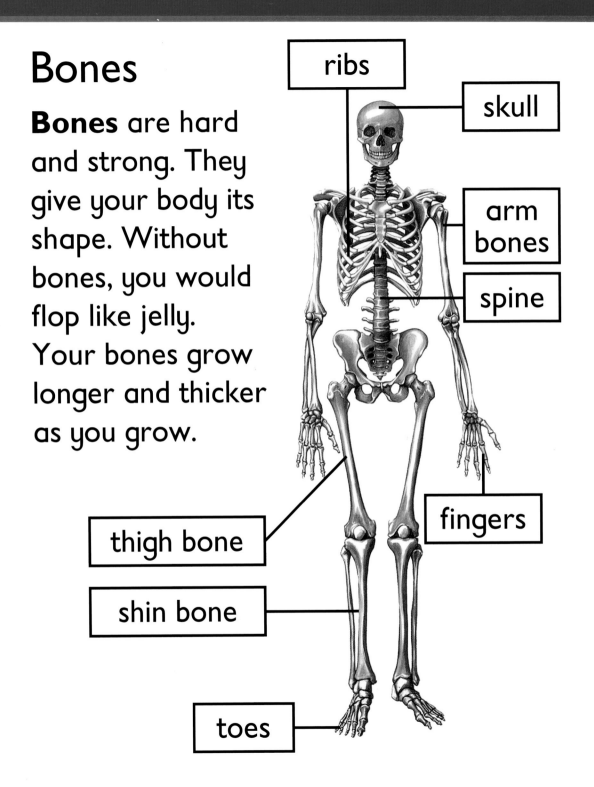

ribs

skull

arm bones

spine

fingers

thigh bone

shin bone

toes

The bones in your **spine** allow you to twist and bend forward and backward. The little girl is bending forward.

Cells

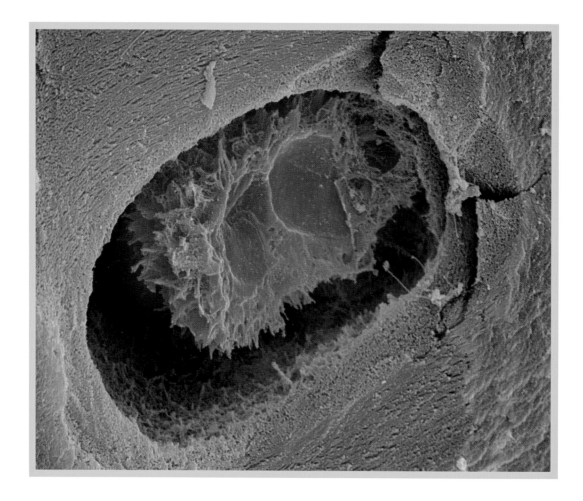

Your body is made up of many different kinds of **cells.** This is a bone cell. Cells are so small that you need a **microscope** to see them.

Cells are like building blocks. Different parts of your body get bigger by adding on extra cells. Your body makes millions of new cells every day.

Two Sets of Teeth

When you were born, your first set of teeth was hidden in your **gums.** They slowly pushed through the gums. A second set formed behind them.

Your first set of teeth begins to fall out when you are about six years old. They are replaced by the bigger teeth from your second set.

Hair and Nails

Hair grows faster than most other parts of your body. Some people let their hair grow long. Others have it cut every few months.

Nails grow quickly, too. They grow from **cells** in the skin. This baby is having her nails cut to keep them from growing too long.

Healthy Food

You need to drink water and eat many kinds of food. These will help you stay healthy and grow strong. Different foods help your body in different ways.

Eating foods with **protein** helps you get the **energy** you need to play. Your body needs protein to grow.

Food that Helps You to Grow

Meat, fish, and eggs contain a lot of **protein.** Cheese and beans contain protein, too. You should eat some protein at every meal.

Bread and rice also contain some protein. If you do not get enough protein, you will not grow very tall.

Food that Helps Your Bones

These foods all help your **bones** grow. They contain **calcium.** Calcium in your bones makes them strong and long.

Calcium also makes your teeth stronger. But you still need to brush your teeth at least twice a day to keep them **healthy.**

Thinking and Learning

As children grow older, they begin to think and learn different things. This young child is learning to use his hands.

As you get older, you can do more difficult things. You also learn to read, write and how to do math. You will never stop learning.

Glossary

bones hard parts of the body underneath the skin and flesh

calcium thing in food that makes your bones and teeth hard and strong

cells very small building blocks that make up the different parts of the body

energy power to move and do things

gums flesh around your teeth

healthy feeling well, with all the parts of the body working properly

height how tall a person is

microscope tool that lets you look at things that are normally too small to see

parents someone's mother and father

protein thing your body needs to build new cells. It is found in some foods.

spine backbone

toddler young child between about one and three years old

More Books to Read

Rowe, Julian. *Watch It Grow*. Danbury, Conn.: Scholastic Library Publishing, 1994.

Tuxwoth, Nicola. *Growing*. New York, N.Y.: Anness Publishing Inc, 1998.

Wilkes, Angela. *See How I Grow*. New York, N.Y.: DK Publishing, 2001.

Index